dear heart,

POESY ROE

Dear Heart,
You Are Magic.

Printed in the United States of America
First printing, 2024

Book cover & interior design by Poesy Roe

www.poesyroe.com
poesyroe.substack.com
instagram.com/frompoesyland

For the tender-hearted dreamers.

For those who color outside the lines.

For my inner child and her relentless devotion to being herself.

For Lilah, Claire & Levi—
Your magic has forever changed me.
Never forget how special you are
and how deeply you are loved.

I wrote this for you.

TABLE OF CONTENTS

PART 1: REMEMBER WHO YOU ARE

PART 2: TRUST YOURSELF

PART 3: BELIEVE IN YOUR MAGIC

PART 4: CELEBRATE YOUR GOODNESS

INTRODUCTION

It's been a little over five years since I sat in therapy and had a revelation about how deeply self-critical I was.

I was drowning in feelings of failure and regret, believing nothing I did was ever good enough. I felt I was behind in life, and I didn't know how to catch up or make up for the laundry list of mistakes I'd made.

I had so many dreams and desires but felt disqualified to pursue any of them. My soul felt crushed.

I knew I couldn't keep living in this loop of self-criticism, sabotage, and punishment, but my brain couldn't posit a solution other than relentless hustling to prove my worthiness (which clearly wasn't working.)

My therapist asked me, "What do you think needs to happen in order for you to move forward?"

As I looked at her, God highlighted her glasses to me, and I said, "I need a lens change."

She asked me what this new lens would look like, and I immediately said, "pink."

In that moment, the song "La Vie en Rose" sprang to mind. The song itself is more about seeing the good and positive side of life, but the message I received in my spirit was that of gentleness, compassion, kindness, acceptance, and unconditional love—all of which happen to be the symbolic attributes associated with the color pink.

As we closed out our session, my therapist and I talked about what living a life with this new pink lens would look like. I pulled out my journal and drew a pair of pink heart-shaped sunglasses and wrote these words around them: nurture, generosity, soft, compassion, permission to be, open, grace-full, allowing, forgiving, accepting. The last thing I did in my session was make a list of the ways I thought I had failed and not met expectations.

Then, on a separate piece of paper, I wrote down a prayer I had written in my journal earlier that week.

It said, "I pray I would feel hope—that I can come home to myself and live at peace in my body, and truly, truly know that beauty (inside and out) is mine —because once I do, I will be unstoppable."

We prayed, and I asked for help in forgiving myself and moving forward in freedom. I ripped up the sheet with my "failures" on it, threw it away, and then my therapist gave me a piece of paper with my journal prayer on it. I exchanged unforgiveness for hope.

Since then, I am doing my best to see myself and those around me through that gentle, soft pink lens. I am not perfect and never will be (which is honestly a hard pill to swallow). For most of my life, I banked on perfectionism keeping me safe, but as I'm sure you know, it's just an illusion. So instead, I do the best I can to offer myself and those around me radical acceptance and unconditional love. This is where my 'dear heart' letters came into the picture.

As I was journaling the week before my therapy session, I had a thought: "What if I just get up every morning and ask my heart what it needs? I listen and then do what it asks." It sounded simple enough, but the practice was harder than I expected. I'd grown up believing my heart wasn't trustworthy, that it was too sensitive and tender to live in the world. Beginning this practice would mean I'd have to change those beliefs—that I'd have to surrender the lies that my heart was a liability and a burden, and begin to embrace the truth that my heart is full of deep wisdom, beauty, and magic.

As I began to write these letters and dialogue with my heart, I was met with acceptance, unconditional love, and celebrations of who I am. No matter what I was feeling, these letters allowed me to carve out space to let myself be heard and seen without judgment.

After a lifetime of blaming my "too sensitive" heart for my pain and need to hide, I was cultivating a relationship based on love and respect. I always started the letters "dear heart," (a reference to a C.S. Lewis quote from *The Chronicles of Narnia*). Sometimes I wrote directly to my heart, sometimes it was as if my heart wrote to me, and sometimes it felt like I was receiving messages from my future self reminding me who I was created to be. Developing this form of communication has been so healing after engaging in years of overly critical and negative self-talk. It's a process, but I'm learning day by day how to soften and let down the drawbridge of my heart.

Last fall, it felt vital for me to place the words *en rose* (French for *in pink*), written in my own handwriting, on my arm. This tattoo is forever a guide to the way I want to see myself, those around me, and the world. I discovered, though misguided, that voice was there to keep me safe the best way it knew how. It was urging me to avoid being different at all costs because it was afraid I'd be rejected and end up alone. When these feelings come up now, I do my best to thank them, but then remind myself that I don't let fear call the shots. These experiences have taught me that we don't need much help pointing out our flaws or where we can improve ourselves, but we do need to be reminded who we were made to be. We need to remember that we are creators, and the Divine gave us gifts to enjoy and share.

That is why I wrote this book—to remind us who we are and how deeply we are loved. These letters and poems started out as mine, and now I offer them to you.

May you find the truth of who you are laced inside the vibrations of each syllable, inviting you to slow down and relish your goodness.

May these words encourage and support you in taking up every inch of your God-given space on this earth.

I pray they will water the soil of your heart, seed your belief in yourself, and bring you blooms of love, joy, compassion, creativity, and beauty.

You are magic, dear heart—never forget it.

♥,
poesy

HOW TO USE THIS BOOK

Like water for the soul, these letters and poems are meant to be savored and felt deep within. I encourage you to speak them aloud, letting the sound of your own voice infuse them with life and meaning.

I imagine this book as one you keep on your nightstand, coffee table, or in a cozy nook of your home. It's something you can begin or end your day with, or pick up whenever you need to ignite your creativity, nurture your heart, or be reminded of the infinite love that surrounds you. The book is divided into four parts:

Remember Who You Are: Reminders of your identity and divine essence.
Trust Your Heart: Words to cultivate confidence in your inner wisdom.
Believe in Your Magic: Encouragement to share your unique gifts.
Celebrate Your Goodness: Inspiration to embrace and celebrate your authentic self.

Let your intuition guide you through these pages. Choose a section that resonates, scan the titles to see where your heart leads, or start at the beginning and move through one letter at a time. Trust that whatever way you choose is right for you.

remember who
you are

You Are Worthy

You are honorable. *Pause.* Let those words sink deep into your bones and explode like confetti in your spirit. You are worthy of being known, celebrated and loved for exactly who you are in *this* moment.

You are worthy of all the dreams and desires you've buried down deep in your heart and you are worthy to take action to make them a reality.

Regardless of your past, present or future circumstances, you are worthy to be a participant in building the life you desire. You were made to enjoy all the magic and majesty this world has to offer. Period.

You don't have to keep doing penance for your mistakes and failures. You are worthy and free to create the life of your wildest dreams right now—this very instant. So, what do you want to create? To experience? Unfetter your heart and let it respond with wild abandon.

Let Yourself Unravel

Let yourself unravel. Let all your defenses crumble. As they fall to the earth, you are safe to emerge. You don't have to hide any longer. You can let yourself be seen, in your beauty and your mess—they're both holy.

Lay down your sword—you don't need defending. You are held by the Creator of all. Let your weary muscles collapse. Let them be mended anew, with great Love and care.

You aren't broken, you've just lost some alignment. You weren't meant to carry that load, and it's taken its toll on your body. But rest assured, you are healing. With each breath you are inhaling love, and exhaling pain. You don't have to be on guard...just play and enjoy this precious life.

You Are More

You are stronger than you think.
Smarter than you think.
Wilder than you think.

You are more.

Let your preconceived notions about who you are and who you aren't dissolve. Trust that your desires are leading you where you want to go.

Let yourself feel—*really feel.*

Stop trying to numb the pain away.

Seek truth and beauty in everything you see, touch, taste and hear. That doesn't mean you can't feel sadness or hurt, it just means you allow yourself to feel it all.

You are a prize jewel with so many facets.
Let yourself continue to seek them and see them as you
buff and shine disillusion away.

You have so much to share, to say. Let it all be done in joy (it will be easier to risk from that appreciative, hope-filled place.)

Deep down you know who you are, dearheart—*show us.*

You Are the Architect

You are the architect of your life.

You are the weaver,
the fabricator,
the master builder.

You get to choose what you create.

You are the artist,
the producer,
the deviser,
the inventor

You design your dreams into reality.

Stay close to the desires bubbling up inside you—
They're looking for a way to be expressed.

Be gentle as you draw up plans and make revisions
over and over and over again.

Such is the process of being a human.
Rest assured—
You're learning.
You're growing.
You're finding your way, dearheart.

Go create the most fantastical life you can imagine.

Made for Magnificence

You weren't made for mundane.

You weren't designed to live a formulaic, drag and drop life.

You were made to expand—to challenge the borders of the status quo.

You are a unique being, and you deserve to life a creative life, fueled by curiosity, play & wonder.

You deserve to live a life *aligned* with the values of your heart.

You weren't made for mundane, dearheart.

You were made for *magnificence.*

Take a Break

It's ok to take a break. It's ok to rest.

In fact, it's more than ok—it's how you were designed.

Your body was created to live in cycles and seasons, for ebb and flow. So take a nap. Go for a walk. Curl up on the couch with your favorite book.

Make space to intentionally slow down. You cannot sustain vitality in your body or spirit if you're constantly in motion.

I know it's hard to give yourself that permission.

Our culture tells us our worth is tied to how much we get done, but it's not true. Your value is set.

Your worth isn't on the line.

Get outside and let the breeze dance across your skin. Witness the majesty of the leaves as they release themselves from the trees.

Remember, *you* are nature too.

Let your body fill with appreciation for life. This sacred vessel moves you through space & time day after day after day.

What a miracle.

Honor your miracle by listening to what it needs. It's doing its best to help you, love you & keep you safe. How will you return the favor?

Do You Remember?

Do you remember what it feels like to take up every inch of space that is you? To feel without shame? To speak without fear? To move your body without judgment?

There is an ancient wisdom in you that does.

An eternal spirit who longs for you to remember the depths of your uniqueness, your power, your beauty.

Are you tuning in to hear it? Or are you scanning the static of the anxious mind? The opinions of others?

Your soul is whispering the truth of who you are in every moment—where will you set the dial?

Your Value is Set

Sometimes it can be easy to lose your bearings–to get
caught up in comparing how you wish things were to
how they actually are.

I'm not here to tell you to ignore your feelings.
I believe feelings are data, and they're always
guiding you to something you need to know.

I am here to remind you of this:
Who you are has value right now.
What you have to say has value right now.
What you create has value right now.
Period. No caveats.

Your value isn't contingent on your past choices, your
job title, the amount of money in your bank account,
your relationship status, or how many followers you
have on social media.

Your value is constant.
Your value lives outside of time–
Treat yourself accordingly.

Love is Sure About You

Love is sure about you.

It is confident and certain of your heart and its goodness.

It has no doubts about who you are.

Wrap yourself up in the lightness and strength of that truth and let it soak into every fiber of your being.

The sureness of who you are is not in question.

Your identity is unwavering.

Your gifts, talents, love, wisdom, joy, and generosity immovable. It's your daily work to line up with that truth and create your life *from* that place of sureness, not *for* it.

There is no better feeling than living under the steady stream of Love. I hope you will give yourself the gift of receiving it (in its many forms) today and every day.

May you be so sure of your sparkle and the deep love
that surrounds you at every moment.

Expand Your Essence

You don't have to chase answers. You don't have to follow the path of those around you. You don't have to fall in line or burn yourself out. You just have to practice being present with the quiet, steady, love-filled voice in your spirit and allow it to encourage you and guide you, moment by moment.

Please know this—even though it can feel like it sometimes, you are not alone.

Allow yourself to be loved and supported by those around you. Allow yourself to be seen. You were never meant to build and live your life alone.

Take a leap and search for the kind of people who will bolster the dreams in your heart.

Find a place to tell your stories, sing your songs, share your poetry and create whatever makes your heart come alive. You deserve it. And the world needs it. But most of all, the world needs your presence—your in-the-moment, tapped in,
genuine presence.

Open your heart wide and be generous with it.

Your Worth Isn't On the Line

Today your mind may be racing about all the things you need to make decisions about and take action on.

You may get caught up in mind games that spew so many logical reasons why things won't work, how your timing is off and how behind you are in life.

You put so much pressure on every step you take to be the "right" one, as if it will save you or prove something about your worthiness.

The truth is, this isn't about making right or wrong choices, it's about being in *alignment* with who you are.

It's about slowing yourself down to hear the ceaseless whispers of the Divine inside you:

"You are loved. You are whole. Your worth isn't on the line no matter what you do or don't accomplish."

You Are Welcome

This is an invitation to pause and remember your goodness, to be present with Love and who are you are in this moment.

No matter where you are in the timeline of your story, I know this: *You are a gift.*

You are full of love, creativity, wisdom and magic.

Even if things are messy and imperfect, even if no one else seems to see it. Your worth is outside time and accomplishments. Your essence is inherent and immovable.

So, welcome Love.

Welcome growth. Welcome vulnerability and courage.
Welcome romance, beauty, and adventure.
Welcome imperfection, curiosity and acceptance.

You don't have to censor your heart.

You don't have to justify your desires and dreams.
You can simply allow them to be.

Be a good host and remind yourself often:
You belong here. You are welcome here.

Open

You were created to feel, to yearn, to be enraptured by beauty.

May you delight deeply in the pleasures of everyday life.
May you entrain your eyes to see them and enjoy every morsel.
May you feel deeply held and rooted in the strength of the earth.
May your heart begin to open, petal by petal, as you turn yourself toward the sun.

You were made to open and share your kaleidoscope of colors, it's in the DNA of your cells. Don't be afraid to show them, for they are your strength, not a weakness.

Lead with delight, joy, play & pleasure.

Let their lightness woo the desires of your heart to the surface where they can be made manifest.

You are ready, my love, to leave the past behind—to tuck it away and put it up on the shelf. It's just a history book now, it's not a map or guide to your future. There is so much goodness in you. So much beauty, so much healing. Believe in that. Meditate on that.

Open my darling.

Open that beautiful heart and let its music spill out wherever you go. Open, open, open so you can receive all the goodness you desire. Open, my love. It is safe here. You are safe here.

Let me show you a new way, a new world.
Little by little, everyday.

Open. Open. Open.

Be Led By Your Design

Be led by your design.
Not opinions,
Cultural norms,
Man-made structures.

None of them compare to you.
To the Spirit-breathed constellation of your soul.

So shine brightly.
Co-create with the galaxies above your head,
The fingertips of those you pass in the street.

Weave your web
Of sound,
Color,
Energy.

Spark forth beauty
From the vast well
Of you, of the *Divine*
Entangled,
In the most sacred dance.

Don't Settle

There is an inner spring that resides deep within you—
an eternal fountain of divine love that wants to saturate
every molecule of you.

It longs to remind you who you are:
brave
strong
courageous
beautiful
and brilliant,
with a heart of gold—
one for the ages.

This Love wants to wash away your fears, doubts, insecurities, and anxieties—any thing that would keep you from moving through the world and sharing your heart with joy.

The miracle of all this: you don't have to earn it. It's *a gift—*
it comes with being human.

Sometimes it can be hard to believe we deserve something so lavish. We often cut off the flow and settle for a trickle when a geyser is available.

Don't settle, dear heart.

Take a deep breath, jump in, and swim in the waters of Love.

Be baptized.
Renewed.
Expanded.

Allow the light of Love to illuminate your spirit and seep into every pore.

trust
your
heart

You Can Trust Yourself

I want to invite you on a new journey. One in which you give up the relentless pursuit of "am I good enough?" and settle snuggly into the truth that you always have been. I want you to feel the seismic shift under your feet as you pivot from hustle and worth-proving to the cradle of love.

This new path is sourced with abundance and there is no competition (because you are on your *own* path.)

All this isn't to say it will be easy to maintain your loyalty and devotion to your life.

You'll often encounter people and situations on the road who question you and invite you to doubt yourself. Stay submerged in the truth of who you are so you can see them coming and plan accordingly. Stay devoted to yourself—*your* body, *your* mind, *your* spirit, *your* purpose, *your* gifts and *your* desires.

There will be hard days that will make you want to quit and take a less complicated, more traveled path. But I beg you to not give into conformity. Instead, quiet yourself and listen for the steady, sure heart beating in your chest and let it guide your path. You can trust yourself, dearheart—you really can.

Steep Yourself in Love

May you let yourself be who you desire to be, the person you *know* you are.

May you steep yourself in love so deeply that it extinguishes the hold of fear.

May you bathe in the richness of life each morning before you set out on the day.

May you open up your heart, spirit and body to receive every bit of goodness it has to give.

May you hand over the keys you use to keep yourself hidden, knowing you are held by the Divine.

May you surrender the lies you use to keep yourself safe at the expense of your soul.

May you never be the snuffer of your own light, but a fan to expand it.

You Are Right On Time

It may not seem like it, but you are indeed growing.

Each and every day you show up and do the best you can to create the life you desire.

Be gentle with yourself as you navigate new terrain, and remember that you are not a puzzle to be solved, but an intricate piece of art unfolding in real time.

Stay present and let your tender roots establish themselves.

I know the inclination is to rush, afraid you'll miss your window of opportunity, but I promise you won't.

Take a moment to breathe deeply and consider what dreams are asking to be birthed in *this* season. Whose time has come?

Give yourself space—don't over-think it.

Slip into the seemingly mundane of your day-to-day and watch things announce their presence in due time.

You aren't behind. *You are right on time.*

No Time is Lost

You aren't behind.
You aren't at a deficit.
You don't have to make up for "lost" time.

Take a breath and get your bearings.
Only *you* know which way is true north for *you*.
Release arbitrary timelines. Stay tuned to the
compass of your heart. You are never lost, just
wandering to find your way.

When you feel restless and aren't sure what to
do next, stop and feel your feet on the ground.

Put your hand on your chest and ask your
heart, "what do you need?" It will always
answer—leading with love, compassion and the
next right step.

You can relax, no time is lost.

You are Brave

You are brave.
You are courageous.
You are on the precipice of something new.

The way you trust your intuition and let the Divine lead you is absolutely beautiful.

Some people in your life can't see that, and it hurts like hell...but onward you march.

You won't let their inability to see distract you from the truth of who you are: wise, creative, teeming with joy, wonder and beauty.

When you have a moment of doubt (which is completely normal), take a deep breath and anchor your feet in the earth.

Trust that peace-filled inner voice of yours—it knows the way to everything you desire.

Your Feelings are Data

You don't have to apologize for your feelings. Sometimes they will seem irrational, be misunderstood, or not make sense to you or others, but that doesn't mean they aren't real or valid.

Your feelings are simply data clueing you into what's going on inside you.

Handle all of them with care—be curious, not judgmental.

Take a breath and step back to see what the root of the emotion may be trying to show you. It could be shining a light on an old (possibly negative) belief you're carrying around—one that's causing you to interpret the situation through a distorted lens.

Whatever you discover, give yourself and those in your life empathy and compassion as you navigate your feelings.

The truth is, an open heart feels really vulnerable. And, while living this way means we open ourselves to pain and heartbreak, it also means we open ourselves to love, beauty and joy.

Stay soft and open. Let yourself experience it all—it's worth it.

Everything Changes

All stories come to an end.

We often try to avoid them, but they arrive just the same...reminding us things ebb and flow, wither and bloom.

Eventually, everything changes.

Change doesn't negate the stories we've written or erase the love, laughter and adventure we've found...it simply shifts it into a new space on the bookshelf of our lives.

Be gentle with yourself when you meet an ending.

Make space for all your feelings.

Remember that sadness, grief, hope and anticipation can live on the same page. I have no doubt you'll find your way forward. You will create new portals and craft fantastical tales you can't even begin to conceive of yet.

I can't wait to watch it unfold. Until then, know this: you are an unequivocal marvel—the most beautiful multifaceted gem. Share every angle and light up this place like only you can.

You Know the Way

You are strong.
You know the way.
Your intuition is fierce and loyal.

Trust her to guide you—she's always leading you toward what you what you need.

Listen close. Grab the hem of her dress. Let her be a torch illuminating the depth and wonder you possess.

Breathe deep. Plant your feet in the knowing that you are held and completely known by the Divine.

Let yourself be showered in the vast love of the universe that created every bit of beauty in you and around you.

There is no separation. You are one in the same.

May you lay down with grace any illusions that would tell you otherwise.

You are *so* deeply loved.

May that truth forever be tattooed in the fabric of your spirit.

Take Your Time

You can take your time.

You aren't meant to transform from caterpillar to butterfly overnight. There's a rhythm to life, to your unfolding.

Day by day, you're opening and letting more sun shine on your face, more love fill up your heart.

You are learning that you have everything you need within you.

You are shedding skins of the past, acclimating to a new way of being. You may feel unsure and unsteady and that's ok. It's ok if you don't know what comes next. It's ok if you're afraid of the unknown.

Everyday is a chance to tune into the heart of Love—to the gracious hand of the universe that invites you to explore all the wonder and beauty it holds.

There is an offering here, to co-create and expand the trust you hold within yourself and the Divine.

It's true, the world needs your voice, your story, but dear heart, you need it too. You need it first and foremost.

You need the vibrations of your voice speaking, singing, shouting your truth. You need the movement, the dancing, the embodiment of emotions that cannot be expressed in any other way.

Set a space and allow it out.
Let it emerge—messy, raw, beautiful.

Take a seat at the table of your life. Weave a new narrative in your heart: it's a joy to express yourself.

You don't have to hide from yourself or anyone else.
It's safe to be seen, dearheart.

Bask in the Light.

Brick by Brick

May you allow your heart to speak, to guide, to surprise and to delight.

May you trust its light within you to open you up and reveal treasures you have yet to see.

May you believe in your infinite and inherent worthiness.

And may you allow yourself to build, brick by brick, the unique heartchitecture to support your dreams.

You are exquisite.
You are ready.
Where is your heart leading?

You Aren't Failing

There is a widening and deepening happening inside you.

You may feel like you're off your axis, but it's just being relocated to a more stable and secure position.

Hold on to what you know to be true.

Though debris is falling and the earth is opening up, threatening to swallow you whole, remember:

You are never alone.
You are deeply loved.

You aren't failing, dearheart—
You're just reorienting.

Let the dust settle and the path will become clear.

Rock the Boat

Life is too short to live in fear. You weren't made to repress your heart's desires and hide your magic. You were made to shine your authentic light into the world. Sometimes that comes with criticism and rejection, but more often our vulnerability is met with warmth, connection, and love.

Consider this your invitation to stop placating the crowd and old wounds that keep you stuck. You are far more than your past or any negative labels someone has thrown your way.

Where do you need to stand up and rock the boat? Maybe even dance, jump overboard, light a match to it or build a whole new one.

You're not here to simply fall in line my friend. You always have the answers inside. Go create your dream life, and don't be afraid to rock the boat as needed.

Come Home

Creativity is waiting for you.

She isn't judging you or keeping her distance.

She's always reminding you what's possible if you will slow down, open your heart and listen.

There is no mountain she wishes you to scale to apologize, make amends for the past, or prove your love and worthiness.

She simply offers an invitation: commune with me.

She is always waiting for you, always singing:

"Come home.
Be with me.
I love you."

Will you let her show you the wonders of your soul?

What Could Be

It's time to get quiet,
Put to bed all that remains undone.
Celebrate the bounty at your table,
Let the rotten fertilize what's to come.

Lay regret, failure, and pain at winter's feet
Let her sew for you a new beginning.

In the stillness she transforms,
Carving new paths in your heart.
A surgeon with the utmost precision,
Clearing a path for more love and vision.

May you trust what seems foreign,
Discover secrets in her snow.

May you take her hand and listen intently,
As you cocoon and dream of what could be.

May you settle snuggly into the dark and unknown,
Trusting She knows the way home.

Are You Ready?

Are you ready to love...
To pour out your heart into the things that light you up?

Are you ready to be heard...
To show up fully and stop tiptoeing around who you are?

Are you ready to be seen...
Like confetti exploding through the world with vibrancy and
vivaciousness?

Are you ready to just *be*...
To abandon people-pleasing and trying to be impressive?

Are you ready to release judgment...
to be the truth of who you are with messy, imperfect ferocity?

Are you ready to *give yourself* a stage...
To play, create, speak from?

You are.
You are.
You are.

Stop waiting.

You are full of jaw-dropping, complex beauty.
Allow it to nourish you and the world around you.
You are ready.

You Don't Have to Rush

"You don't have to rush," winter whispers.

There is plenty of time for you to grow and blossom in the summer sun, but that time isn't now.

Now is the time to sink deep inside and sow the seeds of your dreams. To water them and prepare the land of your heart to bloom.

The work of winter is like the flow of water...in and down. The call of winter is to rest and receive nourishment.

To establish sturdy roots and awaken the hologram of your dreams for the seasons ahead.

Our egos don't like this because the fruit of our devotion can't be seen by others...yet.

Winter invites us to have faith in the unseen work happening below the surface and to trust in the inevitability of Spring.

We watch it happen every year in nature, but we often doubt it within the seasons of our own lives.

So, let me remind you, dearheart—you too, are nature. Your spring (and summer and fall) are inevitable.

Don't rush to get there and miss the glory of winter. It has so many gifts to share. Will you heed its invitation?

Effervescent

You are building something, my love—and building takes time.
There is no rush required (because making it isn't to prove your worth.)

There is just consistent devotion to offer. Offer your passion with
enthusiasm and appreciation and let it grow.

Don't try to wrangle a perfect map or schedule into being.
Let it emerge organically.

Right now your job is to show up at the page and write with devotion and
fervor and not hold anything back.

Go *all in* on what lights you up.

Build portals to new worlds with your words and imagination and action.

Not because someone is standing over your shoulder, but because you
can't not share what's bubbling up inside you.

Let your dreams and desires be only this: *effervescent.*

Flourish With Gentleness

Slow down. There is no race—there is only your unfolding, your own precious expression. Trust that your design will not fail you if you follow it and live into it.

Just as the earth needs softening before it can be seeded, so have you required a season of tilling the inner landscape of your heart.

Now the soil is ready for you to plant the seeds of your dreams and tend to them with the utmost care, patience and devotion.

Don't stomp on these delicate shoots or yell at them to hurry up and grow. Do not insist they bloom like they did in years past.

Instead, speak encouragement over them and remind them of their steadfast identity.

Shower them with love and affection.

Remove anything that would block the sunlight and inhibit their growth.

Allow them to flourish with gentleness into their wild and imperfect beauty.

Ripe With Possibility

Today the air is ripe with possibility.

As spring bursts forth, may you awaken to the potential within you and around you.

May you answer its call to dissolve the past and trust in new beginnings.

May you lay to rest the chatter running on a loop in your mind.

May you put your hands in the dirt and breathe in its fertility.

May you plant seeds of hope, desire, and beauty.

And may you trust that your devotion to tending the garden of your heart will yield a field of breathtaking blooms.

poesy roe

believe
in your
magic

Let Love In

May you know how deeply and utterly magnificent you are.

May the essence that is you rise to the surface and shine without reservation.

May you own your wildness and your desire.

May you let it flow freely to whom you deem worthy to receive it.

May you know in your bones how unbreakable you are—how steady, how secure *within you.*

May you bloom and allow others to marvel at your beauty.

May you laugh from the depths of your soul and become enchanted by everyday magic.

And most of all—may you let yourself be loved.
You deserve to be loved.

Open up the desire and be vulnerable. Allow it to flow.

Let love in, dearheart—it's waiting for you.

You are Beauty-full

You are beauty-full.

You are full of goodness and light, shadows and mysteries, all intricately woven into your unique spirit.

Sometimes you forget this truth when you start comparing yourself to others (friends, family, and even strangers on the internet.)

So, I'm here to remind you, dearheart—you are full to the brim with beauty.

It radiates from your heart and shows up in your smile and the kindness of the words that cross your lips.

You may not always feel good enough, but you are.
You may feel broken, but you aren't.

You are simply growing.

Be a witness to your pain and your joy. Be devoted to feeding your soul with love, laughter and acceptance.

You will inevitably bloom.

Let Her Be

Let her speak, this coming You.

Let her rise and appear and whisper in your ear all the wild and delicious ideas she has in store.

Let her experience never-before-seen adventures, and offer her heart without shame.

Let her build trust in the timing of life.

She *is* blooming.
It's not too late.
Her dreams are not too big.

Lean in and wait.

Before long she will explode like fireworks in the night sky...
a fiery beacon, a guiding force for good.

So, let her be.
Let her build.

Let Love envelop the unknown and every bit of her pain, sorrow, and insecurity.

Let it all be held with reverence and grace, loving her into a deep and vast remembering of who she is and has always been.

Reimagine

Imagine a new world.

One where you wake up everyday and do what you feel inspired to do.

This world isn't a slight upgrade, it's a clean slate.

Reimagine everything.

Lay the past to rest with love and tenderness.

You are worthy to create the life of your dreams *right now.*

Let it all be made new.

Reimagine,
Reimagine,
Reimagine.

Weave it into being day by day, and share it with the world.

Becoming

Fall in love with becoming.

Relish every tiny detail as you watch yourself transform under your fingertips, as you mold and shape and paint, day by day the life you desire.

Delight in your daily acts of devotion, knowing you are expanding and revealing in deeper measure the wonder and beauty within you.

Everyday you are becoming more and more yourself—it's breathtaking to watch.

As you continue to lay down your defenses, know you are completely held by the Divine.

Allow yourself to open up to the flow of the universe and receive, dance and create with the source of life itself.

Cease wrestling with judgment.

Stop carrying the weight of your past, and other things you cannot control. Give back the burdens that were never meant to rest on your shoulders. Let the Divine carry them instead.

It's time to offer your be-ing. It's time to speak, write, photograph, paint, dance, sing, create, host—to build what is in your heart.

We desperately need the particular magic, the lens and life experience of *your* story.

Allow yourself to offer who you are in this moment without reservation, knowing nothing is ever complete or perfect.

You are always expanding and sinking deeper into the truth of who you are.

Your heart deserves a seat at the table, and your community needs the gifts and perspective that only you can bring.

Don't let silence steal one more day...*go make some noise.*

Your Compass

I caught a glimpse of you today. Just for a second, when you thought no one was watching. Your defenses were down, and you let your pain rise to the surface. It pierced your eyes, and cracked your perma-smile. You let your heart feel the tension of a million things battling inside you. And even in the midst of chaos there was some relief, some release.

You've been wrestling with your heart, like it's a beach ball you're trying to keep under water. But it's too hard. And exhausting.

Your heart isn't meant to be hidden away or wrestled into submission. Like a beach ball, it's meant to be buoyant and brightly colored, living on the surface where it can be seen, played with.

I know it can be challenging to surrender to the unknown of life, but isn't trying to control and manipulate things to keep them hidden just as bad, if not worse?

Your heart is your compass. Don't hold it under water and pretend you don't know which way to go. You deserve to feel alive. You deserve to create a vibrant, exciting life that brings you joy & fills your heart with love, but you have to stop drowning out your compass.

You have to trust that the feelings and desires floating to the surface are guiding you closer to who you want to become and the life you desire to build.

Listen to your compass, dearheart and let her lead
the way.

A New Way of Being

May your eyes discover a new way of seeing,
Your heart awaken to a new way of feeling.
May your voice give rise to a new way of speaking,
Your ears receive a new way of hearing.
Let your hands create what you've been dreaming,
Your feet walk steady on the path you're seeking.

Allow your desire to entice.
Lay to rest the linear grind.
Be led by your soul to a new way of be-ing.
Of tasting,
And touching,
Of making,
And feeling.

Expand, dear heart.

Lay to rest the former season.
Your soul is calling for a new way of be-ing.
May you slow to its whispers,
Accept its invitations.

Shed the blooms of yesterday,
Tend with care the soil today.

Life is not a race, but a garden to cultivate.

May you widen your borders,
Bear fruit you didn't know you planted,
And flower with ease into all you imagine.

Petal by Petal

The path to opening your heart requires relentless
self-love. It asks you to be a witness to yourself—
to the love, generosity and deep beauty you exude.

It compels you to pour out your adoration, when all
you can see is a laundry list of flaws.

Love knows the Truth, even when you can't see it.
Love knows you're ready, even though you're afraid.
Love trusts you.

Every day is an invitation to mine your gold and
shower your path with affection.

This is your anchor and safe container.

Open your heart, petal by petal.

Allow yourself to craft a life that delights your soul.

You are worthy of that.
You deserve that.

A Stake in the Ground

Your desires are speaking to you—asking you to hold the tension of the now and not yet. Reminding you the unknown isn't solely a place of fear, it's also a place of possibility, hope & inspiration.

These desires are cues from the narrator (you) saying, "Hey, write *this* story! Don't get stuck in the last one—it's time to move on!"

Remember, your wants and impulses aren't arbitrary-they're signals pointing you toward the life you want to create. Relieve yourself of the expectation that this new world will be immediately and fully formed. Instead, focus on breaking ground and building your dream a day at a time. Allow yourself to truly experience each part of the creation cycle.

I bet if you slow down and listen, you'll find that's all your heart is really asking for—proof of motion and devotion to the things you say you care about.

So, stop being wishy-washy. Put a stake in the ground and show your heart you're committed to bringing your dreams to life.

Stop Waiting

You have to stop
Waiting.
For words to come
Platitudes to fill you up,
A red carpet
To change your mind—
About you.

Alarm bells ring
Wake up,
Confess.
The treasure is already there
Buried in your chest,
In your breath.

Stop searching,
Stop hiding
Contorting,
Compiling lists of why
You can't.

Stop
Waiting.

Before you resign—
Sit down,
Numb out
Turn it up loud,
Listen to the beat
Animating
Knowing
Your frequency dancing
A lullaby of remembering
A new old way of seeing

No more fearful waiting
No more hands-tied, hoop-jumping
Just love taking you by the hand
And saying *this way.*

Do not turn around
Do not look back
The past is fertilizer, not a map.

Let the whispers of naysayers fade to black
As Love puts her hand on the small of your back and says:

This way,
This way,
This way.

A Vast Sea of Possibility

May your eyes awaken to the vast sea of possibility within you.

May the facade of past lives give way to layers, depths, colors, and textures you've yet to uncover.

May you give yourself opportunities to expand the borders of your beliefs about who you are and what you're capable of.

May you allow yourself to be daunted and surprised in the same breath.

May you suspend self-doubt long enough to imagine what you could do, be and have if you only allowed yourself the time and space to grow.

May you be gracious toward yourself and surrender self-protective assumptions.

May you lean into the potential of the unknown with fervor and dwell in the possibility of your magic.

May you find the courage to mine the depths of your prismatic heart and shine like only you can.

Walk Softly Toward Your Dreams

Walk softly toward your dreams.
Handle them with reverence and care.
For they live in a liminal space-
Awakening and sharpening,
Day by day by day.

You do not have to wrestle them to the ground.
You need only open your heart and listen.

Listen-
To their whispers...
Their nudges...
Their songs...
Beckoning you to life.

They have no agenda.
They do not seek accolades.

They only seek to play and share wonder with you-
The wonder of this world, the wonders of your soul.

Allow them to snap you back into the magic of who
you truly are, when disguises crumble and your spirit is free.

A Work of Art

Your life is a work of art. Did you know that? Art isn't just reserved for gallery walls or stage performances, it's a way of living. It's how you craft your world—your home, work, relationships.

You get to decide how to create the kind of story you want to exist in. Fear often invites us to hand over the pen to others. They offer seemingly fool-proof formulas, but 'safe' living quickly turns dull, is ill-fitting, and devoid of your unique color-filled lens.

So, dearheart—are you following someone else's script or writing your own?

Your soul came here to experience the breadth of the humanity—beauty, pain, wonder, growth and loss. Your way of living, your art, is your authentic offering to the tapestry of the planet.

You're not just a character, you're the narrator.

What do you dare say?

Open Your Gifts

May you find the courage to open your gifts.
To traverse the cave of your heart,
Excavate the treasures within.

May you bring them back with open hands.
Offer them freely–
Without posturing,
Bravado,
False modesty.

Be done with covert ops,
On-the-shelf living.

Remember: a gift is received.
(not conjured)

Spread your soul confetti.
Take heart-led leaps.
Open your gifts.
And let your essence be unwavering.

Coalesce

You were made to live as one being.
Each part worthy, valuable.
There is no hierarchy, no pedestal.
Everything belongs.

May you lovingly call all the disjointed and hidden pieces back
together—relinquish any barriers that keep them apart.

May you take the shards and compose them into the most stunning
mosaic—an homage to the unique story that is you.

Release any need to posture.
Simply reflect your design.
Play your sacred instrument,
Here and now.

Coalesce.
Coalesce.
Coalesce.

Clear the Decks

Let it get quiet.
Let time come undone.
Let silence greet you–
As a lover who can't get enough.

Bask in the recesses...
Of your imagination.
Ask questions.
Excavate lies.
Plant seeds.
Deep, deeper, deepest.

Let change come.
Don't block the view.
Reclaim your mind,
Kill the clutter you design.

"Clear the decks."
A divine whisper.
"What do you think once the world has gone silent?
 Where will you go when you let go of compliance?"

Clear the decks, love.
Stand naked in your skin.
Clear the decks, love.
You weren't meant to be hidden.

No Matter What

Do not equate your worthiness with your mistakes.

Instead, see them for what they are: part of the creative process, part of being a human soul in a complex atmosphere.

The truth is we cannot control everything floating in our airspace, but we can control how we show up. We can control the words we speak.

We can choose how well we love, and the opportunities we allow ourselves to have when (especially when) we don't feel totally ready and know we won't do it perfectly.

That is when we must remind ourselves that perfection is an illusion, and perfection doesn't invite connection.

At the end of the day our hearts are seeking authenticity–the good, the bad and the ugly. It's all a part of who we are and our experience here.

So, let your wild ideas fill you with hope.

Let your heart be like a balloon cascading across the skyline.

Enjoy the view as long as you have it. And don't judge yourself when you inevitably make your way back to the ground to start the process over again.

You are loved no matter what.

I See You

I see you working so hard—to learn, to grow, to reach your potential. You're giving it everything you've got, and you deserve to celebrate.

So, just for a moment slow down. Savor this moment in time. Look around and take in the beauty at your fingertips. Let it enchant you and bring a smile to your face.

This life, *your life*, is a thing of beauty. It's your own personal work of art.

Maybe in this moment it's not the most aesthetically pleasing. Perhaps there is a pile of wreckage and you are in the midst of transforming it.

Nonetheless, it is still beautiful. *You are still beautiful.*

For beauty is not static, it's dynamic—an ever-changing form with a steadfast, immovable essence containing the multitudes of the universe—just like you.

Take it all in. From the earth to the cosmos, let its majesty envelope your heart and awaken you to the vastness of your soul.

You contain more magic than you can comprehend.

Keep showing up and sharing your stardust with the world.
I see you and I am so proud of you.

Take the Reins

You are in charge of your life.

You know what is best for you (because *you* are in tune with the divine life force energy inside you.)

You are wise beyond your years.
You can be trusted to take the reins.

May you learn to live by faith, not fear.

May you learn how to live each moment with joy and contentment with who you are. May you let all disillusions dissolve and only the truth of who you are remain.

Weed and water the garden of your life with tender care.

Live with unrelenting devotion to the seeds of magic in your soul—do not deprive them of what they need to grow and thrive.

Bathe them in abundance.
Bathe them in grace.
Bathe them in beauty.

Activate their light with your love and watch as they illuminate your path home.

celebrate
your
goodness

You

You are divine.
You are held.
You are made of fire.

From the depths you've risen to ignite the light in your heart
and it will not depart from you.

You've made friends with your shadow and welcomed her into
your heart.

Healing is happening, even if you can't yet feel it or see its fruit.

The mysteries of the Divine are dancing over you and through
every cell of your being.

I bless you to receive it and welcome it with an open heart.

I bless you to take ownership of your desires.

And finally, I bless you to see unequivocally through the eyes of
Love exactly *who* you were designed to be.

You are Goodness.
You are Light.
You are Love.

Scoop every ounce of this truth into your spirit, and
give yourself permission to *be* who you've *always* been.

May it be anchored in your body and spirit always.

And so it is.

Irreplaceable

Amidst the chaos and noise of the world, I want you to know this: *You are an irreplaceable thread in the tapestry of humanity.*

Irreplaceable.

Your story matters.
Your voice matters.
Your art matters.
Your work matters.
YOU *matter.*

You make a difference everyday, whether you know it or not.

These days it can be easy to pick apart your 'thread' when it doesn't look like the ones you see on social media and in pop culture. But, if humanity is to remain a diverse, vibrant tapestry then we need different sizes, colors, and textures of thread. We need the contrast to create a whole picture of what it is to be human.

Keep sewing your light into the fabric of humanity and leaving a trail of beauty everywhere you go.

This place wouldn't be the same without you.

Rebirth

It's time for rebirth...
To flap your wings with ferocity.
To split the chrysalis wide open,
and sing the song of your soul.

The past has dissolved.
Your form has changed—
don't apologize for it.

Don't tiptoe around who you are—proclaim it.

Flutter your wings and dance across azure skies and the
delicate petals of spring.

Come alive, delight your heart, and all who have eyes to
see your soulful beauty.

Gold to Mine

Your soul is voracious fire.
It longs to burn bright–
Free of misguided expectations.

Stoke its flames with love and intention.
Breathe in the goodness and depth you hold.
Make space to hear and be heard amidst the noise.

Seek the pleasure of everyday delights.

Get drunk on beauty.
Surrender time that has expired,
Embrace what is in front your face.
Believe your heart is worthy of what you seek.

Enliven your imagination.
Dance with desire.
Dream with wildness.

You need to create.
The world needs your creations.
It's time to start building.

There's gold to mine in that heart of yours.
What are you waiting for?

Play

"The opposite of play isn't work, it's depression."
-Stuart Brown

Play ignites the magic of your soul.

In play there is no calculating or planning, just pure fun and expression.

It's a gateway for your essence to flow out unfiltered.

It's medicine from your heart reminding you who you are deep down (without the opinions of others or stresses of life.)

The truth:
You are an incandescent ball of light.
You are joy incarnate.
You are Love.

When you stop playing you rob yourself of yourself.

Create space to be light-hearted and have so, so, so much fun.

It's vital to your to your wellbeing, even if you can't measure it with the typical metrics of "productivity" and "success."

You deserve time to play, dearheart–take it.

Speak Well

Speak well–
Of your heart,
To your heart.
Of the memories made,
And the ones confined to your imagination.

Speak well–
To your past, your present, your future.
To your fumbles, your victories,
Your embarrassments,
To your hopes, your desires,
Your spectacularly outlandish dreams.

Do not be overcome by the outside voices.
Listen to what's buried inside.

Allow the Truth to bubble up with ease,
Offer a soft spot for your heart to land.

Love is not a taskmaster.
Love is an invitation...
Expand your borders,
Relish your goodness.

Deep, soul-nourishing change is in
your hands, your mind, your mouth.

Speak well to your iridescent soul.
Speak well to your lonely shadows.
Speak well to the path you are painting.

Speak well,
Speak well,
Speak well.

You Are Easy to Love

Your beauty runs deep and wide.

Your joy is infectious.

It is a privilege to swim in the ocean of your heart.

You are worthy of so much affection
(*you should never have to wonder about that.*)

You deserve to be loved fiercely.

You don't have to control or manipulate things to receive it.

Don't settle for crumbs.

You deserve a full meal—*a feast of love.*

I'm so proud of who you are.
You are transforming and you can't even see it yet.

Stay with yourself no matter what.
Continue to affirm the beauty and goodness that is you.

You are easy to love.

There is Space For All of You

May you move through this day in truth and honesty with Love as your foundation.

May you not sideline the feelings that are hard or ugly.

May you make space for *every* piece of you that wants to be heard. And may you lean forward with an attentive ear to what is being said.

There is space for all of you.

The doubter and the believer, the sad and the joyful, the heartbroken and the healed.

Grace, grace, grace.

May you swim in rivers of deep grace as you navigate life in this earthly vessel.

There is goodness here.
Entrain your eyes to see it and hold its gaze.

You are blessed.
You are a blessing.
May you never forget it.

Permission Granted

May you allow yourself to...

Be a beginner.
Mess up.
Pursue your dreams.
Travel the world.
Speak your truth.

Stop self-sabotaging.
Let yourself be seen.
Make art.
Dance.

Open your heart.
Make mistakes.
Figure it out as you go.
Leave the past behind.

Grow.
Build community.
Laugh uncontrollably.
Rest.

Create.
Fall in love.
Change your mind.

Accept yourself as you are.
Ask questions.
Disagree.

Buck the status quo.
Be misunderstood.
Make yourself proud.

Be *you.*

Don't hold yourself hostage.

You are enough.
You are worthy.
Enjoy your life now.

Yours is the only permission you need.

Let Yourself Be Seen

Let yourself be seen in all ways, not just those you deem acceptable. Let yourself be seen in your messiness and be loved anyway.

You waste so much energy when you try to hide and suppress what you deem ugly and unloveable. What if it all belonged? What if there was nothing so "ugly" it couldn't be met with compassion?

This is your work to do—to love ALL the parts of yourself-physically, mentally, emotionally...to not put yourself in boxes or segmented parts, but to see the whole of who you are and to love all of you unconditionally.

It's the work of a lifetime, so stop looking for the finish line. Lean into the landscape of right now and see where it takes you, what it inspires you to study and create, who it connects you to.

Let go of the illusion that safety is outside the borders of your body. Safety lives inside you, because 'safety' is Love and your ties to it can never be severed.

No matter how you may feel in any given moment, you are held, loved and contained by the vast and exquisite presence of the Divine Love that created you.

Rest in that.

You Cannot Be Replaced

There is only *one* you.

You cannot be replaced.
You cannot be duplicated.
Your light cannot be extinguished.

Remember that when you want to slink back
 into your shell and hide.

Contrary to the story you often tell yourself,
The absence of your presence is felt—*deeply.*

The symphony of the universe hums differently
without the magical vibrations of *your* voice.

Yours is a weighty contribution.
Don't make light of it—
Joyfully accept it.

Allow the essence of you to be *completely free.*

When you do, you mirror to every soul you meet the
rich and deep reservoir of love, goodness and beauty
within them.

You Are Poetry

You are poetry, dearheart—
Your own free-form meter.

It doesn't require explanation.
It simply gets to *be*...floating on the wind,
Finding its way into the hearts of those who need it.

Stop creating charts and graphs to justify its worthiness.
It's incalculable. Like trying to quantify the beauty of a rose,
The magic of the cosmos.

You're meant to express,
Be experienced...
Period.

Let yourself loose,
Like a wild horse running down the beach.
Take in the salt air,
The majesty of all that surrounds you.

Look for fellow travelers with the same wildness in their chest.
Let it bond you.

Journey unknown terrain together,
Driven by the passion, honor and bliss
Of being alive,
Of being you.

WRITE YOUR OWN DEAR HEART LETTER

Writing letters to your heart is a gentle practice of self-connection and loving dialogue. These letters create a sacred space where you can meet yourself with acceptance, understanding, and unconditional love. Sometimes you might write directly to your heart, sometimes your heart might write to you, and sometimes it might feel like wisdom flowing from divine guidance or your future self.

Begin each letter with "Dear Heart," and let the words flow naturally. There's no wrong way to write these letters. You might share your dreams, acknowledge your feelings, celebrate your progress, or simply check in with what your heart needs today. The key is to write from a place of self-acceptance and compassion, leaving judgment at the door.

Your heart has deep wisdom to share when given the space to speak. Through these letters, you can begin to trust that wisdom and cultivate a relationship with yourself based on love and respect.

Use the pages that follow to compose your own dear heart letters, or grab your favorite journal and begin your practice there.

dearheart,

dearheart,

ABOUT THE AUTHOR

Poesy Roe has a deep love for beauty and soul-stirring words. She fills her days with vibrant colors, long walks in nature, and impromptu dance parties around her home in Nashville, TN. Ever the hopeless romantic, she often sings along to the enchanting melodies of Ella & Louis records while making dinner.

More than anything, she loves to soak up and reveal the beauty of people and places—whether through her pen, music, camera, or makeup brushes. Her magic lies in reminding people who they are and helping them express their creativity and beauty.

She believes with every fiber of her being that you are magic. Your design is intentional. Your essence is the one-of-a-kind poetry that we need in the world. Poesy hopes the words you find here will encourage and inspire you to listen to the creative nudges of your heart and follow them with devotional, wild abandon.

To sign up for Poesy's weekly *Dearheart Mail* visit her Substack at poesyroe.substack.com.

ACKNOWLEDGMENTS

To the loyal readers of *Dearheart Mail*–your love & support over the past 4 years paved the way for this book to become a reality. Thank you for believing in me and reading my words week after week.

My family–Thank you for giving me space to grow & find my voice. You fill my heart with so much love and inspiration. I love you to the moon and back.

Ashley R–Thank for holding my dear heart with so much care and letting me cry in coffee shops all over Nashville. Your love and belief in my dreams has transformed me.

Karen, Liza & Cynthia–Your steadfast love and support has birthed a deeper belief in myself. Thank you for being a safe space to share my heart. I couldn't do life without you.

Heather P–You are a rare human. Thank you for relentlessly encouraging me (and everyone you meet) to create and share their voice. Knowing you & being a part of your community has changed my life.

Ash, Emily, Kat, LT, Tara & Lindsey–Thank you for staying after me to write a book! I am so lucky to have had such incredible friends for 30+ years. Seahorses, for-eva!

Abby-Pie–Whether near or far, you're one of my dearest friends and biggest cheerleaders. Thank you for believing in my creative gifts & *insisting* I share them. Your whimsical heart inspires me to dream big.

Jess- Your warmth and generosity of spirit is a blessing to me and the world. Thank you for endlessly supporting my dreams. You are a rare gem.

Melea- Your playful spirit inspires me to be more light-hearted and not take myself so seriously (apricots! apricots!) Thank you for the many times you've helped me move through self-doubt and share my voice.

Eryn-Your love and support have been a bolster these past 10 years. Thank for creating with me, believing in me and loving me so well.

Sarah C- Thank you for believing in me and my words. Your wisdom, love and friendship are a treasured gift.

Maria B-You are a true soul friend. Thank you for sharing your voice with me--truly the best medicine for my body & spirit.

Ana- Thank you for being a listening ear & reminding me of the truth when I forget it. Grateful for you & Jiro!

Dearest Reader,

Thank you so much for taking the time to read my book and support my work--it truly means the world to me.

I'd also like to invite you to visit Poesyland--my creative playground on Substack where I share my writing, art, and music, as well as inspiration and practices for living an authentic, heart-led life.

My hope is this magical place will transform the way you see yourself, and allow you to explore your deepest dreams and desires.

Scan the QR code below to enter and begin your journey through Poesyland. See you soon.

♡,
poesy